15-Minute
FOODIE

More than 50
Fast Recipes for Kids

by Megan Borgert-Spaniol

CAPSTONE PRESS
a capstone imprint

Table of Contents

Food in 15!

Are you looking for simple recipes that are tasty and filling? Whether you're coooking up a meal, a snack, a dessert, or something special for a party, this book is full of ideas to satisfy your cravings. And the best part is, these recipes come together in 15 minutes or less! So grab your kitchen supplies and read through the tips on the next page. Soon enough, you'll be a 15-minute foodie!

Basic Supplies

blender	mixing bowls
cheese grater	nonstick skillet
colander	spatula
cooking pot with cover	toaster
knife and cutting board	tongs
measuring cups and spoons	whisk

Kitchen Tips

Ask an adult for permission before
you make a recipe.

Read through the recipe and set out all ingredients
and supplies before you start making.

Using metric tools? Use the conversion chart below
to make your recipe measure up.

Wash your hands before and after you handle food.
Wash and dry fresh produce before use.

Ask an adult for help when using a knife, blender,
or stovetop. Wear oven mitts when removing items
from the microwave.

When you are done making food, clean your
work surface. Wash dirty dishes and put
all supplies and ingredients back
where you found them.

Standard	Metric
¼ teaspoon	1.25 grams or milliliters
½ teaspoon	2.5 g or mL
1 teaspoon	5 g or mL
1 tablespoon	15 g or mL
¼ cup	57 g (dry) or 60 mL (liquid)
⅓ cup	75 g (dry) or 80 mL (liquid)
½ cup	114 g (dry) or 125 mL (liquid)
⅔ cup	150 g (dry) or 160 mL (liquid)
¾ cup	170 g (dry) or 175 mL (liquid)
1 cup	227 g (dry) or 240 mL (liquid)
1 quart	950 mL

Breakfast Parfait

Start your day with this tasty treat. Packed with protein and fiber, it's good for you too!

Ingredients

1½ cups quick oats
3 tablespoons vegetable or coconut oil
2 tablespoons maple syrup
½ teaspoon cinnamon
¼ teaspoon salt
½ cup yogurt
½ cup fresh fruit, chopped if needed

Supplies

measuring cups and spoons
mixing bowl
rubber spatula
large nonstick skillet
baking tray
serving glass

1. Pour the quick oats into the mixing bowl. Add the oil, maple syrup, and cinnamon to create granola. Use the rubber spatula to mix the granola together.

2. Heat the skillet over medium heat. Carefully pour the granola into the skillet and spread it in an even layer.

3. Stir the granola when the bottom layer begins to turn golden brown. Stir periodically until all the granola is golden brown. Then turn off the heat.

4. Spread the granola into a thin layer on the baking tray to help it cool. Sprinkle the salt over the granola.

5. Add ½ cup granola to the serving glass. Layer about ⅓ of the yogurt and ⅓ of the fruit on top. Repeat the layers twice more. Breakfast is ready!

Banana Oat Pancakes

Whip up some super simple pancakes
for a relaxing morning at home.

Ingredients

1 banana
1 egg
1 tablespoon milk
1 tablespoon vegetable oil
½ cup rolled oats
½ teaspoon baking powder
¼ teaspoon cinnamon
¼ teaspoon salt
fruit, chocolate chips, or other toppings (optional)

Supplies

blender
measuring cups and spoons
large nonstick skillet
spatula

1. Put the banana, egg, milk, vegetable oil, rolled oats, baking powder, cinnamon, and salt in the blender.

2. Blend everything together until the batter is smooth. Then heat the skillet over medium heat.

3. Pour ¼ cup of batter onto the hot skillet to make each pancake. Try to fit three or four pancakes on the skillet at a time.

4. When small bubbles appear on the pancakes, flip them with the spatula. Cook the pancakes for about one minute more, or until the bottoms are golden brown.

5. Remove the cooked pancakes from the skillet and repeat steps 4 and 5 with the remaining batter. If you'd like, top your pancakes with fruit, chocolate chips, or other toppings of your choice!

Egg & Cheese
English Muffin

This classic egg-and-cheese combo makes for a hearty breakfast or lunch. All you need is a toaster and microwave!

Ingredients

¼ teaspoon oil
1 egg
salt and pepper
1 English muffin
1 tablespoon mayonnaise
hot sauce (optional)
1 slice cheddar cheese

Supplies

measuring spoons
microwave-safe bowl
  or mug
paper towel
fork
cutting knife
toaster
spreading knife

1. Pour the oil into the microwave-safe bowl. Use the paper towel to spread the oil around the bottom and sides of the dish.

2. Crack the egg into the dish. Beat the egg with the fork. Season the egg with a pinch of salt and pepper.

3. Microwave the egg for 30 seconds. If the center is still runny, microwave it for another 15 seconds. Then let the egg cool. While the egg cooks and cools, slice and toast the English muffin.

4. Spread mayonnaise over the English muffin halves. If you'd like, add a few drops of hot sauce.

5. Place the slice of cheddar cheese and the cooked egg onto an English muffin half. Top with the other half. Breakfast (or lunch) is served!

BLTA Wrap

Take a crispy, juicy, salty lunchtime favorite to a new level with creamy avocado.

Food Tip

Squeeze lime juice over leftover avocado before storing it in a covered container. This helps keep the avocado from turning brown!

Ingredients

2 strips bacon
1 tablespoon mayonnaise
1 tortilla
lettuce leaves
tomato slices
salt and pepper
1 avocado

Supplies

microwave-safe plate
paper towels
measuring spoon
spreading knife
knife and cutting board
spoon
toothpick (optional)

1. Line the microwave-safe plate with two layers of paper towels. Place the bacon strips side by side on top of the paper towels. Place another paper towel on top of the bacon strips.

2. Microwave the bacon for two minutes. If it isn't crispy, continue cooking for 15 seconds at a time until it is. Let the bacon cool.

3. Spread the mayonnaise over the tortilla. Place three or four lettuce leaves across the middle of the tortilla.

4. Place three or four tomato slices on top of the lettuce. Season the tomato with a pinch of salt and pepper.

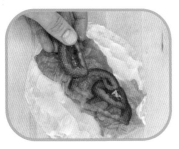

5. Chop the cooled bacon strips into smaller pieces and sprinkle them over the tomato.

6. Cut the avocado in half and remove the pit. Cut the fruit into thin slices while it's still in the peel. Then scoop a few slices out of the peel and place them on top of the bacon.

7. Wrap the sides of the tortilla over the filling. If you'd like, use a toothpick to secure the wrap. Remove the toothpick when you're ready to dig in!

Toaster Panzanella

Hunks of warm bread join cool, crunchy vegetables in this chopped salad of Italian origin.

Food Tip

Traditional panzanella calls for stale, dry bread that can better soak up the dressing. In this recipe, it's okay if your bread isn't stale—the toaster will help dry it out.

Ingredients

2 slices white bread
1 tablespoon mayonnaise
6 to 8 cherry tomatoes, halved
¼ cup chopped bell pepper
¼ cup chopped red onion
¼ cup chopped cucumber
2 tablespoons olive oil
1 teaspoon balsamic vinegar
salt and pepper
¼ cup fresh mozzarella pearls, quartered

Supplies

toaster
measuring cups and spoons
spreading knife
knife and cutting board
mixing bowl
small bowl
whisk
spoon

1. Toast the bread slices until they are golden. Spread mayonnaise over each slice and set them aside.

2. Use your hands to gently toss the tomatoes and vegetables together in the mixing bowl.

3. In the small bowl, whisk together the olive oil and balsamic vinegar. Season with a pinch of salt and pepper.

4. Drizzle the oil and vinegar over the salad.

5. Cut the bread slices into bite-size pieces and add them to the salad along with the mozzarella pearls.

6. Use the spoon to gently toss the salad so all ingredients are evenly distributed. Your panzanella is ready to enjoy!

Ranch Chicken Quesadilla

Layer chicken, greens, and cheese between two golden tortillas for this tasty and filling meal!

Ingredients

2 flour tortillas
½ cup cooked shredded chicken
1 tablespoon ranch dressing, plus more for drizzling
½ cup fresh spinach
⅓ cup shredded mozzarella

Supplies

large nonstick skillet
measuring cups and spoons
spatula
knife and cutting board

1. Place one tortilla in the skillet. Spread the chicken on the tortilla and pour the ranch dressing over it.

2. Cover the chicken with the spinach and mozzarella.

3. Place the second tortilla over the fillings. Then place the skillet on the stove over medium heat.

4. Check the color of the bottom tortilla after about three minutes. When it is golden, carefully flip the quesadilla in the skillet.

5. Cook the quesadilla for another two minutes or until the bottom tortilla is golden.

6. Transfer the quesadilla to a cutting board and cut it into triangles. Serve the quesadilla with a drizzle of ranch dressing!

Tuna Pasta

This delicious seafood pasta can be served hot or cold.

Ingredients

2 green onions, chopped
1 can tuna, drained
¼ cup mayonnaise
½ tablespoon lemon juice
salt and pepper
6 ounces dried pasta
  (shell, penne, or similar)
1 cup peas

Supplies

cooking pot with cover
knife and cutting board
measuring cups and
  spoons
mixing bowl
mixing spoon
colander

1. Fill the pot with water. Cover and heat it on the stove over high heat until the water comes to a boil.

2. Combine the green onions with the tuna, mayonnaise, lemon juice, and a pinch of salt and pepper in the mixing bowl.

3. When the water boils, add a pinch of salt and the dried pasta to the pot. Stir the pasta and turn the heat down to medium high. Cook the pasta according to the box's instructions.

4. When the noodles are cooked, turn off the heat and add the peas to the pot. Stir for 20 seconds before draining the pasta water with the colander.

5. Pour the cooked noodles and peas back into the pot. Add the tuna mixture and stir to combine. Season with salt and pepper as desired before you dish up your meal!

Taco Scoops

Thanks to the firm ribs that run down their centers, romaine lettuce leaves make sturdy, crunchy scoops that are perfect for taco fillings!

Ingredients

½ tablespoon olive oil
½ pound lean ground beef or turkey
1 teaspoon ground cumin
½ tablespoon chili powder
¼ teaspoon garlic powder
¼ teaspoon onion powder
½ teaspoon salt
½ cup tomato sauce
1 bunch romaine lettuce, chopped into leaves
⅓ cup shredded cheese
⅓ cup diced tomato
¼ cup diced red onion

Supplies

large nonstick skillet
spatula
measuring cups and spoons
knife and cutting board

1. Heat the oil in the skillet over medium-high heat. Add the ground meat and cook for about five minutes, breaking up the meat as it cooks.

2. When the meat is browned, add the cumin, chili powder, garlic powder, onion powder, and salt. Pour in the tomato sauce and stir to combine everything.

3. Turn down the heat to medium low and continue cooking the meat for another five minutes.

4. Scoop the ground meat into the romaine leaves. Top the meat with the shredded cheese, tomato, and onion. Your taco scoops are ready to eat!

Personal Pizza

Flatbreads like pita or naan are the perfect size for personal pizzas. How will you top yours?

Food Tip
Feel free to add or swap in your favorite pizza toppings, such as onion, feta, or even pineapple!

Ingredients

pita or naan bread
$\frac{1}{3}$ cup marinara sauce
4 to 6 olives, sliced
$\frac{1}{4}$ cup chopped bell
  pepper
7 to 10 pepperoni slices
$\frac{1}{2}$ cup shredded
  mozzarella
salt and pepper (optional)

Supplies

toaster or nonstick
  skillet
measuring cups
spoon
knife and cutting board

1. Heat the bread in the toaster or skillet over medium-high heat until it is crisp and golden.

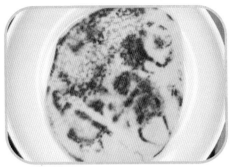

2. Spread the marinara sauce over the bread using the spoon. Leave the edge of the bread uncovered.

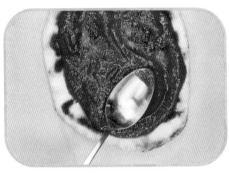

3. Add the olives, peppers, and pepperoni slices to the pizza.

4. Top the pizza with shredded mozzarella. Then microwave the pizza for 20 seconds at a time until the cheese is melted. Season with salt and pepper if you'd like. Bon appétit!

Broccoli Mac 'n' Cheese

All you need is four main ingredients and a big cooking pot for this classic comfort dish.

Food Fact!

Packaged shredded cheese has ingredients that keep it from clumping. Because of this, it doesn't melt into sauces well.

Ingredients

4-ounce block sharp cheddar cheese
salt and pepper
6 ounces dried pasta (elbow, shell, or similar)
2 cups chopped broccoli
¾ cup heavy cream

Supplies

cooking pot with cover
cheese grater
measuring cups
mixing spoon
knife and cutting board
colander
whisk

1. Fill the pot with water and cover it. Heat it on the stove over high heat until the water boils. While you wait, shred the cheddar with the cheese grater.

2. Add a pinch of salt and the dried pasta to the boiling water. Stir the pasta and turn the heat down to medium high. Cook the pasta for five minutes less than the cook time on the box.

3. When the pasta is done cooking, add the broccoli to the pot. Cook the broccoli and pasta together for two to three minutes before draining the water with the colander.

4. Pour the heavy cream into the pot and heat it over medium-high heat, whisking frequently. When the cream starts to simmer, whisk in the shredded cheddar. Continue whisking until the cheddar is fully melted.

5. Pour the pasta and broccoli back into the pot and stir to coat everything in sauce. Season the pasta with salt and pepper to your liking. Then serve it up!

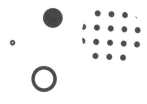

Creamy Tomato Soup

Canned tomato soup does the job, but why not make your own with a few pantry staples?

Ingredients

2 tablespoons olive oil
½ cup chopped white
 onion
2 cloves garlic, chopped
½ teaspoon salt
28-ounce can crushed
 tomatoes
2 cups vegetable broth
½ cup heavy cream, plus
 more for serving
black pepper

Supplies

measuring cups and
 spoons
cooking pot
knife and cutting board
mixing spoon
blender
serving bowl

1. Heat the olive oil in the pot over medium-high heat. Cook the onion and garlic in the oil for about three minutes, stirring occasionally. Season with the salt.

2. Pour the pot's contents into the blender along with the tomatoes and vegetable broth. Blend the soup, pausing every five seconds to lift the cover and release any steam.

3. Pour the soup into the pot and bring to a simmer. Stir the soup frequently for about five minutes.

4. Stir the heavy cream into the soup. Season with black pepper as desired. Pour the soup into the serving bowl and add a drizzle of heavy cream!

Loaded Baked Potato

Make a warm, filling meal out of one humble potato and a few delicious toppings!

Ingredients

1 large russet potato
1 tablespoon butter
1/3 cup shredded cheddar
  cheese
1 tablespoon sour cream
1 tablespoon bacon bits
1 green onion, chopped

Supplies

fork
microwave-safe plate
knife and cutting board
measuring cups and
  spoons
spoon

1. Poke the potato several times on each side with the fork. Place the potato on the microwave-safe plate and microwave it for five to six minutes.

2. Let the cooked potato cool for two minutes. Then cut it in half lengthwise.

3. Fluff up the cooked potato with the fork. Spread the butter on the potato halves. Then sprinkle the shredded cheddar over the potato.

4. Place a dollop of sour cream onto each potato half.

5. Top the potato halves with the bacon bits and green onion. Then dig in!

Food Fact!
Poking holes in a potato allows steam to escape while the potato bakes. Without steam holes, the potato could explode!

29

Pad Thai

This delicious noodle dish requires some multitasking, but it's worth the extra effort!

Ingredients

2 tablespoons vegetable oil
2 tablespoons soy sauce
1 tablespoon fish sauce
2 tablespoons lime juice, plus wedges for serving
1 tablespoon brown sugar
6 ounces pad thai rice noodles
1 teaspoon butter
2 eggs
salt and pepper
¼ cup chopped peanuts
2 green onions, chopped

Supplies

cooking pot with cover
whisk
measuring cups and spoons
small bowl
stirring spoon
microwavable bowl
colander
tongs
knife and cutting board

1. Fill the pot with water and cover it. Heat the pot over high heat until the water boils. While you wait, whisk together the oil, soy sauce, fish sauce, lime juice, and brown sugar in the small bowl. Set the bowl aside.

2. When the water boils, turn off the heat and add the noodles to the pot. Stir to separate the noodles. Then let them cook in the hot water for six to eight minutes.

3. Grease the microwavable bowl with the butter. Crack the eggs into the bowl. Whisk them with a pinch of salt and pepper.

4. Microwave the eggs for 20 seconds at a time, whisking between intervals, until the eggs are cooked.

5. Drain the cooked noodles and pour them back into the pot. Add the eggs and sauce to the pot. Gently toss everything together with the tongs.

6. Toss the peanuts and green onions with the noodles. Serve your pad thai with a lime wedge!

Decked-Out Pretzels

These funky pretzels are the perfect blend of sweet, salty, and crunchy!

Food Fact!
Adding oil to chocolate helps it melt to a smooth and shiny consistency.

Ingredients

1 cup white chocolate chips

1 tablespoon coconut or vegetable oil

1 cup dark chocolate chips

pretzels

chopped nuts

sprinkles

Supplies

measuring cups and spoons

microwave-safe bowls

spoons

forks

tray or baking pan

parchment paper

1. Pour the white chocolate chips and ½ tablespoon oil into a microwave-safe bowl. Microwave the chocolate in 25-second bursts. Stir between each one until the chocolate is melted and smooth.

2. In a separate bowl, repeat step 1 with the dark chocolate chips and the remaining oil.

3. Place pretzels in each bowl of melted chocolate. Use the forks to cover the pretzels with chocolate.

4. Remove the pretzels from the bowls using the forks. Tap the forks against the bowls to remove excess chocolate. Place the pretzels on a tray or baking pan lined with parchment paper.

5. Use a fork to drizzle dark chocolate on the white chocolate pretzels. Then drizzle white chocolate on the dark chocolate pretzels.

6. Sprinkle chopped nuts and sprinkles over the pretzels before the chocolate sets. Put the pretzels in the freezer for five minutes or until the chocolate hardens. Enjoy your pretzel snack!

Chili Cheese
Popcorn

Buttered popcorn is a solid snack, but chili powder and grated Parmesan cheese take it to the next level!

Food Fact!
Steam makes popcorn chewy. Partially uncovering the pot to let steam escape helps keep popcorn crisp.

Ingredients

2 tablespoons coconut or
  vegetable oil
½ cup popcorn kernels
4 tablespoons butter
1 teaspoon chili powder
½ teaspoon salt
1 cup grated Parmesan
  cheese

Supplies

measuring cups and
  spoons
large pot with lid
small microwave-safe
  bowl
whisk
large bowl
rubber spatula

1. Pour the oil into the large pot. The oil should coat the bottom of the pot. Toss two popcorn kernels into the oil. Cover the pot. Heat the oil on the stove over medium-high heat until one of the kernels pops.

2. While waiting for the test kernels to pop, put the butter in the small microwave-safe bowl. Microwave it for 15 seconds at a time until melted. Whisk in the chili powder and set the butter aside.

3. When a test kernel pops, uncover the pot. Pour in the remaining kernels so they evenly cover the bottom of the pot. Cover the pot.

4. When the kernels start to rapidly pop, partially uncover the pot so steam can escape. When the popping slows down, take the pot off the heat.

5. Pour half the popcorn into the large bowl. Top with half the salt, half the Parmesan cheese, and half the chili butter. Toss with the rubber spatula.

6. Add the remaining popcorn, Parmesan, and chili butter to the bowl. Toss with the rubber spatula. Enjoy your snack!

Nutty Cracker Stacks

Coat layers of flaky cracker and smooth nut butter in chocolate to make this irresistible snack!

Ingredients

nut butter
butter crackers
1 cup chocolate chips
½ tablespoon coconut or
    vegetable oil
sea salt (optional)

Supplies

spreading knife
tray or baking pan
parchment paper
measuring cups and
    spoons
microwave-safe bowl
spoon
fork

1. Spread a thin layer of nut butter over two crackers. Stack the crackers. Place a third cracker on top.

2. Repeat step 1 to make more cracker stacks. Place them on a tray or baking pan lined with parchment paper. Put the tray in the freezer.

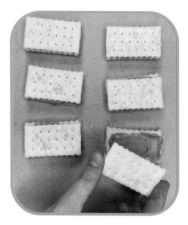

3. Pour the chocolate chips and the oil into the microwave-safe bowl. Microwave the chocolate in 25-second bursts. Stir between each one until the chocolate is melted and smooth. Take the cracker stacks out of the freezer.

4. Place a cracker stack in the bowl. Use a spoon to cover the stack in chocolate.

5. Remove the stack from the bowl with a fork. Tap the fork against the bowl to remove excess chocolate. Place the covered stack back on the lined tray.

6. Repeat steps 4 and 5 with the remaining stacks.

7. If you'd like, sprinkle sea salt over each cracker stack. Put the stacks in the freezer for five minutes so the chocolate sets. Your sweet and salty snacks are ready to eat!

Cheese Stick Roll-Ups

Dress up your cheese sticks with a duo of sweet jam and salty meat.

Ingredients

deli-sliced salami or ham
jam
cheese sticks

Supplies

measuring spoons
spreading knife
knife and cutting board
toothpicks

1. Lay flat a few pieces of salami or a piece of deli-sliced ham.

2. Spread 1 teaspoon jam over the meat.

3. Place a cheese stick along the edge of the meat. Roll the cheese up in the meat.

4. Repeat steps 1 through 3 to make additional roll-ups. Then slice each roll-up into quarters.

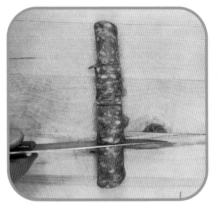

5. Use toothpicks as skewers for easy snacking!

Southwest Dip

This protein-packed dip is full of fresh flavors
and a bright kick of lime!

Ingredients

1 can corn
1 can black beans
1 large tomato, diced
1 small red onion, diced
1 avocado, diced
salt
1 teaspoon lime juice
tortilla chips

Supplies

colander
medium bowl
measuring cups
  (optional)
knife and cutting board
spoon
measuring spoons

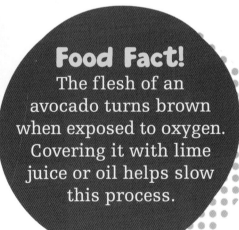

Food Fact!
The flesh of an avocado turns brown when exposed to oxygen. Covering it with lime juice or oil helps slow this process.

1. Drain and rinse the canned corn and black beans. Pour them into the medium bowl.

2. Add the diced tomato and onion to the bowl.

3. Cut the avocado in half and remove the pit. Slice the flesh of the fruit into small cubes while it's still in its peel. Scoop the cubes into the bowl with a spoon.

4. Sprinkle a pinch of salt and the lime juice into the bowl. Stir so everything is well mixed.

5. Serve the dip with tortilla chips!

Parmesan Crisps

A quick turn in the microwave transforms shredded Parmesan cheese into cheesy, crunchy crisps.

Ingredients

Parmesan cheese
black pepper (optional)

Supplies

grater
measuring cups
large microwave-safe
  plate
parchment paper
measuring spoons

1. Grate the Parmesan cheese until you have 1 cup.

2. Line the plate with parchment paper.

3. Scoop four 1-tablespoon piles of shredded Parmesan onto the plate. The piles should be well-spaced so they won't melt into each other.

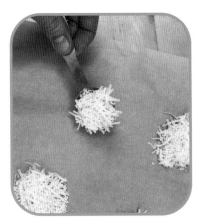

4. Microwave the Parmesan piles for 50 seconds. If you'd like, sprinkle black pepper over each crisp.

5. Repeat steps 3 and 4 with any remaining Parmesan. Then munch your crunchy snack!

Homemade Hummus

This easy hummus recipe packs loads of flavor!

Food Tip

Experiment with the amounts of olive oil, lemon juice, garlic, and salt to suit your taste. Just remember to add a little at a time, and take a taste before adding more!

Ingredients

1 can garbanzo beans
   (chickpeas)
3 tablespoons olive oil
2 tablespoons water
2 tablespoons lemon juice
1 clove garlic, minced
½ teaspoon salt
chips, carrots, or other
   snacks for dipping

Supplies

colander
blender
measuring spoons
knife and cutting board
rubber spatula
serving bowl

1. Drain and rinse the canned garbanzo beans. Pour them into the blender.

2. Add the olive oil, water, and lemon juice to the blender.

3. Put the garlic and salt in the blender.

4. Blend everything together until it is smooth.

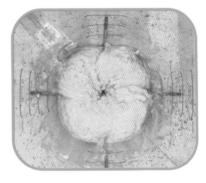

5. Use the rubber spatula to transfer the hummus to the serving bowl. Serve it with chips, carrots, or other snacks for dipping.

Cheesy Grape Bites

These sweet, tangy, crunchy bites make for a refreshing snack!

Ingredients

½ cup cream cheese
2 tablespoons sour cream
red and green grapes
½ cup chopped walnuts

Supplies

2 small bowls
measuring cups and
 spoons
whisk
skewers
tray or large plate

1. In a small bowl, whisk together the cream cheese and sour cream until the mixture is smooth.

2. Pour the chopped walnuts into the other small bowl.

3. Place a grape on a skewer. Roll the grape in the cream cheese mixture.

4. Roll the grape in the bowl of chopped walnuts until the cream cheese is covered. Place a second grape on the same skewer. Place the grape skewer on the tray or large plate.

5. Repeat steps 3 and 4 to make more grape bites!

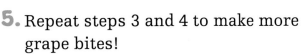

Avocado Toast

Cool, creamy avocado meets warm, buttery toast in this delicious snack. Add a crunchy vegetable for texture!

Ingredients

½ tablespoon butter
bread
avocado
salt and pepper
sliced cucumber or radish
(optional)

Supplies

small skillet
spatula
plate
knife and cutting board
spoon

1. Heat the butter in the small skillet over medium heat.

2. When the butter is melted and bubbling, place a slice of bread onto the skillet. Let it cook for one minute.

3. Use the spatula to check the bread's underside. When it's golden brown, flip the bread. When both sides are golden brown, turn off the heat and transfer the bread to the plate.

4. Cut the avocado in half and remove the pit. Cut the fruit into thin slices while it's still in its peel. Scoop out the slices with a spoon and lay them on the toast.

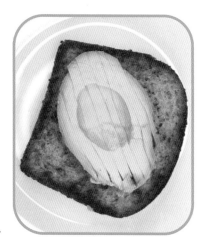

5. Fan out the avocado on the toast and lightly sprinkle it with salt and pepper. If you'd like some crunch, lay thin slices of cucumber or radish over the avocado.

Granola Poppers

These nutty, oat-filled bites are like cookies that you don't have to bake!

Ingredients

2 tablespoons honey
1/3 cup peanut butter
1/4 cup shredded coconut
1 cup rolled oats
1/4 cup semisweet
   chocolate chips
salt

Supplies

large mixing bowl
measuring cups and
   spoons
mixing spoon or rubber
   spatula
plate or tray

1. In the large mixing bowl, combine the honey, peanut butter, and shredded coconut.

2. Add the rolled oats, semisweet chocolate chips, and a big pinch of salt to the bowl. Mix everything together.

3. Roll 1-tablespoon portions of the granola mixture into balls. Place them on the plate or tray.

4. Put the granola balls in the freezer for five minutes before enjoying.

Tuna Pepper Boats

Cuts of crunchy bell pepper carry creamy tuna salad like boats sailing straight to your belly.

Food Fact!
Red bell peppers are the sweetest variety, followed by orange, yellow, and green.

Ingredients

1 can tuna (5 ounces)
2 tablespoons mayonnaise
salt and pepper
red bell pepper

Supplies

small mixing bowl
measuring spoons
spoon
knife and cutting board

1. Drain the canned tuna and put it in the small mixing bowl.

2. Add the mayonnaise and a pinch of salt and pepper to the tuna. Stir to combine everything.

3. Cut the red bell pepper in half. Cut out the white parts and stems.

4. Fill each pepper half with the tuna mixture.

5. Cut each filled pepper half into two pieces. Top the pepper boats with a sprinkle of salt and pepper!

Rainbow Bagel

Slice up a rainbow of fruit to make a colorful bagel that's anything but boring.

Ingredients

bagel

assorted fruits in colors of the rainbow (for example, strawberries, cantaloupe, pineapple, kiwi, blueberries, grapes)

cream cheese

Supplies

knife and cutting board

toaster (optional)

spreading knife

1. Slice the bagel in half if it isn't already. If you'd like, toast the halves and let them cool.

2. Cut the fruit into thin slices.

3. Spread cream cheese over each bagel half.

4. Arrange the fruit on top of each bagel half to make a colorful, rainbow-inspired design!

Sunny Smoothie

Send your taste buds to a tropical beach with this refreshing banana-orange smoothie!

Food Tip
To make this a non-dairy smoothie, try a dairy-free yogurt made of coconut or almond milk. You can also add creaminess with avocado or nut butter.

Ingredients

1 sliced banana
½ cup orange juice
¼ cup vanilla yogurt
4 or 5 ice cubes

Supplies

blender
knife and cutting board
measuring cups
drinking glass

1. In the blender, combine the banana, orange juice, and yogurt.

2. Add ice cubes to the blender.

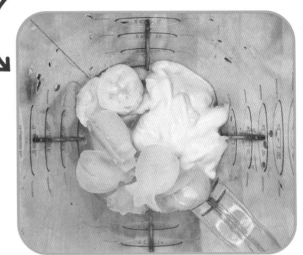

3. Blend everything until smooth. Pour the smoothie into a glass to serve.

Guacamole
for a Group

No party is complete without a big bowl
of this classic Mexican dip.

Ingredients

4 ripe avocados
¼ cup chopped red onion
2 teaspoons lime juice
¼ teaspoon sea salt
1 bag tortilla chips

Supplies

knife and cutting board
spoon
mixing bowl
measuring cups and
  spoons
fork
serving bowl

Food Tip

Squeeze lime juice over leftover guacamole before storing it in a covered container. This helps keep the guacamole from turning brown!

1. Cut the avocados in half and remove the pits. Scoop the avocado halves into the mixing bowl.

2. Add the diced onion, lime juice, and sea salt to the bowl.

3. Mash all the ingredients together with the fork. Keep stirring and mashing until the guacamole is creamy.

4. Scoop the guacamole into the serving bowl. Serve with tortilla chips!

Pineapple Pecan Cheese Ball

Spread a scoop of this crunchy-creamy cheese on anything and everything!

Food Tip
Leave out the pecans in this recipe for a nut-free snack.

Ingredients

8-ounce softened cream cheese block

¼ cup chopped green onions (about 3 or 4 green onions)

¼ cup canned crushed pineapple

⅓ cup shredded cheddar cheese

¼ teaspoon sea salt

1 cup chopped pecans

crackers and vegetables for dipping

Supplies

mixing bowl

mixing spoon

electric mixer (optional)

knife and cutting board

measuring cups and spoons

parchment paper

tray

serving plate and spreading knife

1. Place the cream cheese block in the mixing bowl. Use the mixing spoon or the electric mixer to beat the cream cheese until it is soft and creamy.

2. Add the green onions, crushed pineapple, cheddar, salt, and ¼ cup chopped pecans to the bowl with the cream cheese.

3. Mix everything together with the spoon. Then press the mixture into a ball. Put the bowl into the freezer for a few minutes to solidify the ball.

4. Spread the remaining chopped pecans on a tray lined with parchment paper. Roll the cheese ball in the pecans. Transfer it to the serving plate. Place crackers, pretzels, and vegetables on the plate. Use the spreading knife to serve your delicious creation!

Cool & Creamy Veggie Dip

Crunchy vegetables need creamy dip. Skip the store-bought stuff and make your own!

Ingredients

¾ cup plain Greek yogurt
¼ cup mayonnaise
1 teaspoon dried dill
1 teaspoon garlic salt
½ teaspoon onion powder
vegetables for dipping

Supplies

measuring cups and
  spoons
mixing bowl
whisk
serving bowl

1. Whisk the Greek yogurt and mayonnaise together in the mixing bowl.

2. Add the dried dill, garlic salt, and onion powder to the bowl.

3. Whisk everything together until the dip is smooth and uniform. Then transfer the dip to the serving bowl and serve with vegetables!

Crunchy Cucumber Bites

These crispy, juicy, salty, and creamy bites
will be a new party favorite.

Ingredients

½ cup softened cream
 cheese
½ cup ricotta
½ tablespoon lemon juice
½ teaspoon sea salt
¼ teaspoon black pepper
1 sliced cucumber
12 cherry tomatoes,
 halved

Supplies

measuring cups and
 spoons
mixing bowl
electric mixer (optional)
mixing spoon
whisk
knife and cutting board
serving tray

1. Put the cream cheese in the mixing bowl. Use the electric mixer or mixing spoon to beat the cream cheese until it is soft and creamy.

2. Add the ricotta, lemon juice, sea salt, and black pepper to the bowl. Whisk everything together.

3. Scoop about ½ tablespoon of the cream cheese mixture onto each slice of cucumber.

4. Top each cucumber with a tomato half. Then place your bites on the tray and serve them!

Nacho Mountain

Your guests will have no trouble conquering the crunchy, cheesy peak of this nacho mountain.

Ingredients

¾ cup canned black beans
1 bag tortilla chips
up to 2 cups shredded
    cheddar cheese
1 small tomato, diced
¼ cup diced red onion
1 cup shredded iceberg
    lettuce
¼ cup sour cream

Supplies

colander
large microwave-safe dish
measuring cups
knife and cutting board
spoon
plastic bag (optional)
scissors (optional)

1. Drain and rinse the black beans. Set them aside.

2. Arrange a layer of tortilla chips in the microwave-safe dish. Top the chips with a generous sprinkling of shredded cheddar and about ¼ cup of the black beans.

3. Add another layer of tortilla chips on top of the first. Make this layer a little smaller than the first. Top it with more shredded cheddar and black beans.

4. Continue layering chips and toppings, making each layer of chips smaller so the stack forms a mountain. As the layers get smaller, use less cheese and black beans.

5. Once the mountain is constructed, microwave it for 20 seconds at a time until the cheese is melted.

6. Sprinkle the tomato, onion, and lettuce on top of the nacho mountain.

7. Add dollops of sour cream to the nacho mountain. Or place a scoop of sour cream into a plastic bag and cut off the bag's corner. Then pipe a sour cream swirl onto the nacho mountain!

Sandwich Skewers

How do you make a classic meal more interesting?
Deconstruct it and stick it on a skewer!

Food Tip
Feel free to add or swap in other favorite sandwich toppings, such as peppers, cucumbers, or lettuce.

Ingredients

crusty bread, such as a
   baguette or ciabatta
block of cheese, such
   as Swiss, cheddar, or
   Monterey Jack
sliced salami
cherry tomatoes
baby pickles

Supplies

knife and cutting board
wooden skewers
serving tray

1. Cut the bread into 1-inch (2.5-centimeter) cubes and the cheese into ½-inch (1.3-cm) cubes.

2. Stick a skewer through one bread cube. Slide the bread cube three-quarters of the way down the skewer.

3. Add a cube of cheese, a folded slice of salami, a cherry tomato, and a baby pickle to the skewer. Space the ingredients evenly along the skewer.

4. Finish the skewer with one more cube of cheese and bread. Then place the skewer onto the serving tray.

5. Repeat steps 2 through 4 to make more sandwich skewers!

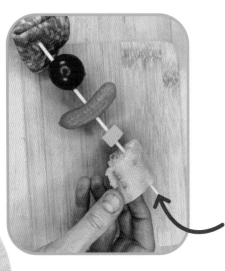

Cheese Fondue

Get out the grater! Freshly shredded cheese is best for this easy microwave fondue.

Food Fact!
The word *fondue* comes from the French verb *fondre*, which means "to melt."

Ingredients

8-ounce block Swiss cheese
4-ounce block medium cheddar cheese
1 cup heavy cream
2 tablespoons apple juice
2 teaspoons cornstarch
salt and pepper
vegetables, cubed bread, and other foods for dipping

Supplies

cheese grater
measuring cups and spoons
microwave-safe bowl
whisk
serving bowl
wooden skewers or toothpicks

1. Grate the blocks of Swiss and cheddar cheese. Set the shredded cheese aside.

2. Pour the heavy cream and apple juice into the microwave-safe bowl. Microwave for 30 seconds at a time, whisking between intervals, until the cream is hot.

3. Whisk the shredded cheese and cornstarch into the hot cream. Microwave the mixture for 30 seconds at a time, whisking between intervals, until the cheese is fully melted. Be patient! It will take several heating intervals for the cheese to fully melt.

4. Season the cheese with salt and pepper to your liking. Then pour the fondue into the serving bowl. Use the wooden skewers or toothpicks to dip vegetables, cubed bread, and other foods in the fondue!

Coney Dog Sliders

Give new form to the Coney Island hot dog, a beef frank topped with meat sauce, yellow mustard, and onion.

Food Tip
Each hot dog makes two sliders. Divide the number of sliders you want to make by two, and that's how many hot dogs and buns you'll need! One can of chili will make up to 16 sliders.

Ingredients

1 can beef chili
  (15 ounces)
fully cooked beef hot dogs
hot dog buns
yellow mustard
1 white onion, diced

Supplies

microwave-safe bowl
  and plate
spoon
paper towels
knife and cutting board
measuring spoons
serving tray

1. Empty the can of beef chili into the microwave-safe bowl. Cover the bowl with the microwave-safe plate. Microwave the chili for 60 seconds. Stir and microwave for another 60 seconds. Then set the chili aside.

2. Wrap one to two hot dogs in a paper towel and put them on the microwave-safe plate. Microwave the hot dogs for 60 seconds and remove them from the plate. Repeat with the remaining hot dogs.

3. Place each hot dog into a bun. Then cut the hot dogs in half.

4. Pour about 1 tablespoon of chili over each hot dog.

5. Squirt a ribbon of yellow mustard over each chili dog. Then sprinkle about 1 teaspoon of the diced onion over each chili dog.

6. Arrange your Coney dog sliders on the serving tray!

Loaded Puppy Chow

Take traditional puppy chow to the next level by adding a mix of sweet and salty ingredients.

Food Tip

Do you or a member of your party have a peanut allergy? Swap in almond butter instead of peanut butter and cashews instead of peanuts.

Ingredients

1 cup semisweet
  chocolate chips
½ cup peanut butter
1 tablespoon butter
7 cups crispy corn and
  rice cereal
2 cups powdered sugar
2 cups pretzels
1 cup peanuts
1 cup candy-coated
  chocolates

Supplies

measuring cups
butter knife
microwave-safe bowl
large mixing bowl
rubber spatula
serving bowl

1. Pour the chocolate chips, peanut butter, and butter into the microwave-safe bowl. Microwave the mixture in 25-second bursts. Stir between each one until the mixture is melted and smooth.

2. Pour the crispy corn and rice cereal into the large mixing bowl. Pour the melted chocolate mixture over the cereal. Use the rubber spatula to gently stir the mixture to coat the cereal.

3. Sprinkle ½ cup powdered sugar over the cereal. Stir the mixture gently with the rubber spatula.

4. Repeat step 3 three more times to add a total of 2 cups powdered sugar.

5. Add the pretzels, peanuts, and candy-coated chocolates to the bowl. Gently toss everything together and pour your loaded puppy chow into the serving bowl!

Frozen Banana Bar

Guests will love dipping and decorating
their own custom banana pops!

Ingredients

3 bananas

toppings such as shredded coconut, nuts, pretzels, candy-coated chocolates, and sprinkles

¾ cup chocolate chips

1 tablespoon coconut or vegetable oil

Supplies

knife and cutting board

chopsticks or craft sticks

parchment paper

tray

bowls

spoons

measuring cups and spoons

microwave-safe bowl

1. Peel the bananas and cut each one in half. Push a stick into each banana half.

2. Place the bananas on a tray lined with parchment paper. Put the tray in the freezer while you prepare the toppings and chocolate.

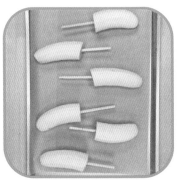

3. Prepare the toppings. Chop toppings such as pretzels or nuts into smaller pieces. Then place each topping in its own bowl with a spoon.

4. Pour the chocolate chips and oil into the microwave-safe bowl. Microwave the chocolate in 25-second bursts. Stir between each one until the chocolate is melted and smooth.

5. Place one spoon in the bowl of melted chocolate and set it next to the toppings you prepared. Take the banana popsicles out of the freezer. Invite guests to dip and decorate their bananas and place them back onto the parchment-lined tray.

6. Put the tray back in the freezer for five minutes so the chocolate sets. The banana pops are ready to serve!

Monster Cookie Balls

No eggs, no flour, no sweat! These yummy no-bake cookie balls will be ready in no time!

Ingredients

1 cup chunky peanut butter

1 tablespoon honey

2 tablespoons maple syrup

salt

1 cup rolled oats

½ cup candy-coated chocolates

½ cup semisweet chocolate chips

Supplies

mixing bowl and spoon

measuring cups and spoons

parchment paper

tray

1. Combine the peanut butter, honey, maple syrup, and a pinch of salt in the mixing bowl.

2. Add the rolled oats, candy-coated chocolates, and semisweet chocolate chips to the bowl. Mix everything together.

3. Roll 2-tablespoon portions of the mixture into balls. Place the balls on a tray lined with parchment paper.

4. Put the tray in the freezer for five minutes. Then serve your treats!

Confetti Popcorn

Sweet and salty meet under a rainbow of confetti in this party-perfect treat.

Food Fact!

Steam makes popcorn chewy. Partially uncovering the pot to let steam escape helps keep the popcorn crisp.

Ingredients

3 tablespoons coconut or
  vegetable oil
½ cup popcorn kernels
½ teaspoon sea salt
1 cup white chocolate
  chips
¼ cup rainbow sprinkles

Supplies

measuring cups and
  spoons
large pot with lid
mixing bowl
microwave-safe bowl
rubber spatula
parchment paper
tray

1. Pour 2 tablespoons oil into the large pot. The oil should coat the bottom. Toss two kernels into the oil and cover the pot. Heat the oil on the stove over medium-high heat until one of the kernels pops.

2. When a kernel pops, uncover the pot and pour in the remaining kernels. Cover the pot again.

3. When the kernels start to rapidly pop, partially uncover the pot so steam can escape. When the popping slows down, take the pot off the heat. Pour the popcorn into the mixing bowl and toss with the sea salt.

4. Pour the white chocolate chips and 1 tablespoon oil into the microwave-safe bowl. Microwave the chocolate in 25-second bursts. Stir between each one until the chocolate is melted and smooth.

5. Pour the melted chocolate over the popcorn. Mix with a rubber spatula.

6. Pour the popcorn onto a tray lined with parchment paper. Add the rainbow sprinkles to the popcorn.

7. Put the tray into the refrigerator for five minutes so the chocolate sets. Then serve your colorful popcorn!

Raspberry Sherbet Punch

A big bowl of fizzy, creamy punch doubles as a centerpiece for your table of party goodies.

Ingredients

6 cups raspberry
    lemonade
6 cups lemon-lime soda
10 scoops raspberry
    sherbet
½ cup raspberries

Supplies

measuring cups
punch bowl or large
    mixing bowl
ice cream scoop or large
    spoon
ladle

1. Pour the raspberry lemonade and lemon-lime soda into the punch bowl.

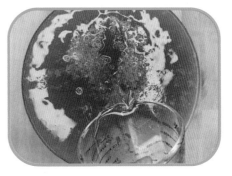

2. Add the scoops of sherbet to the bowl.

3. Sprinkle the raspberries on top of the sherbet scoops in the bowl. Then add the ladle for serving!

PB&J Cups

You can't beat the classic sweet-and-salty combo of peanut butter and jelly—unless, of course, you add in chocolate!

Food Tip
This recipe calls for peanut butter, but any nut butter will work!

Ingredients

1 cup semisweet chocolate chips
2 teaspoons coconut or vegetable oil
¼ cup peanut butter
2 tablespoons jam

Supplies

measuring cups and spoons
microwave-safe bowl
spoon or rubber spatula
cupcake liners

1. Pour the chocolate chips and oil into the bowl. Microwave the chocolate in 25-second bursts. Stir between each one until the chocolate is melted and smooth.

2. Scoop ½ tablespoon melted chocolate into a cupcake liner. Gently shake the liner to spread the chocolate across the bottom. Repeat with three more liners.

3. Place the liners in the freezer for two minutes.

4. Take one liner out of the freezer. Spread 1 teaspoon peanut butter over the chocolate. Then spread ½ teaspoon jam on top of the peanut butter.

5. Top the cup with 1 tablespoon melted chocolate. Put the cup back in the freezer.

6. Repeat steps 4 and 5 with the other cups. Freeze the cups for few minutes before enjoying!

Warm Cinnamon Apples

This comforting mix of fruit and spice makes for a cozy treat.
Enjoy it as is, or pair it with something cool and creamy!

Ingredients

1 apple
1 teaspoon sugar
¼ teaspoon cinnamon
¼ teaspoon cornstarch
½ tablespoon water
heavy cream, ice cream,
  or yogurt (optional)

Supplies

apple peeler or paring
  knife
knife and cutting board
microwave-safe bowl
whisk
measuring spoons
spoon or rubber spatula
microwave-safe plate
serving bowl

1. Peel the apple. Cut the flesh off the core in large chunks. Cut the chunks into slices about ¼ inch (0.6 centimeters) thick.

2. In the microwave-safe bowl, whisk together the sugar, cinnamon, cornstarch, and water.

3. Add the apple slices to the bowl and stir to coat them with the mixture.

4. Cover the bowl with the microwave-safe plate. Microwave the apples for two minutes. Then let the apples cool for two minutes.

5. Transfer the apples to the serving bowl. If you'd like, top them with heavy cream, ice cream, or yogurt!

Coconut Macaroons

Dark chocolate chips bring bittersweet balance to sweet coconut in this simple dessert.

Food Fact!

Adding oil to chocolate helps the chocolate melt to a smooth and shiny consistency.

Ingredients

2 cups shredded coconut
4 tablespoons plus
  1 teaspoon coconut oil
2 tablespoons maple
  syrup
½ cup dark chocolate
  chips

Supplies

mixing bowl
measuring cups and
  spoons
spoon or rubber spatula
plate or tray
parchment paper
microwave-safe bowl

1. In the mixing bowl, combine the shredded coconut, 4 tablespoons coconut oil, and the maple syrup.

2. Scoop 2 tablespoons of the coconut mixture and form it into a ball. Place the ball on a plate or tray lined with parchment paper. Keep making balls until the mixture is gone.

3. Put the coconut balls in the freezer while you prepare the chocolate.

4. Pour the chocolate chips and 1 teaspoon coconut oil into the microwave-safe bowl. Microwave the chocolate in 25-second bursts. Stir between each one until the chocolate is melted and smooth.

5. Take the coconut balls out of the freezer. Drizzle a spoonful of melted chocolate over each coconut ball.

6. Put the coconut balls in the freezer for a few minutes so the chocolate sets. Then enjoy your coconut macaroons!

Watermelon Slushie

Cool off on a hot summer day with this sweet, tart, and icy drink.

Ingredients

2 cups cubed ripe
  watermelon
1 teaspoon sugar
1 teaspoon lime juice
1 heaping cup ice cubes

Supplies

knife and cutting board
measuring cups and
  spoons
blender
serving glass

1. Pour the watermelon cubes into the blender.

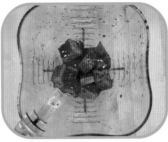

2. Add the sugar and lime juice to the blender. Blend everything together for 5 to 10 seconds.

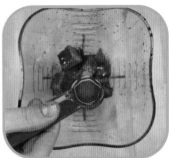

3. Add the ice cubes to the blender. Blend until the drink reaches a slushie consistency.

4. Pour the slushie into the serving glass and enjoy!

Food Fact!

The spot on the underside of a melon is called its field spot. Ripe melons have butter-yellow field spots. Unripe melons usually have white spots.

Chocolate Fondue

This super simple microwave fondue
will have you dipping in no time!

Food Fact!
The word *fondue*
comes from the
French verb *fondre*,
which means
"to melt."

Ingredients

½ cup dark chocolate chips

½ cup milk chocolate chips

¼ cup heavy cream

1 teaspoon coconut or vegetable oil

marshmallows, cookies, fruit, and other treats for dipping

Supplies

measuring cups and spoons

microwave-safe bowl

serving bowl

tray

wooden skewers

1. Pour the dark chocolate chips and milk chocolate chips into the microwave-safe bowl. Add the heavy cream and oil to the bowl.

2. Microwave the chocolate in 25-second bursts. Stir between each one until the chocolate is melted and smooth.

3. Pour the melted chocolate into the serving bowl. Place the bowl on the tray with wooden skewers, marshmallows, cookies, fruit, and other treats for dipping!

Rainbow 'Mallow Bites

Fruity cereal brings bright pops of
color to this time-tested treat.

Ingredients

vegetable oil
10-ounce bag
  marshmallows
4 tablespoons butter
3 cups plain crispy rice
  cereal
3 cups fruity crispy rice
  cereal

Supplies

microwave-safe bowl
rubber spatula
knife for cutting butter
large mixing bowl
measuring cup
spoon
baking pan

1. Grease the microwave-safe bowl and rubber spatula with the oil. Pour the marshmallows into the bowl and add the butter.

2. Microwave the marshmallow mixture for 30 seconds at a time. Stir with the greased rubber spatula after each interval until the mixture is melted and smooth.

3. Grease the large mixing bowl. Combine the plain crispy rice cereal and fruity crispy rice cereal in the bowl. Stir until the cereals are well-mixed.

4. Pour the melted marshmallow over the cereal. Use the greased spatula to combine everything.

5. Grease the pan. Pour the cereal mixture into the pan and use the greased spatula to spread it out evenly.

6. Put the pan in the freezer for a few minutes to cool before serving!

Choco-Berry Salad

Food Tip
If you don't have an electric mixer, whip your cream with a whisk. It will take a little longer, so work with a helper so your arm doesn't get too tired!

Tart berries, sweet cream, and bursts of bittersweet chocolate come together in perfect harmony in this dessert salad.

Ingredients

3.4-ounce package instant vanilla pudding mix
1½ cups milk
1 cup heavy cream
1 cup raspberries
1 cup blueberries
¾ cup dark chocolate chips
caramel topping (optional)

Supplies

mixing bowls
measuring cups
whisk
electric mixer
rubber spatula
serving bowls

1. In a mixing bowl, combine the pudding mix with the milk. Whisk until the pudding gets thick. Put the bowl in the refrigerator while you whip the cream.

2. Pour the heavy cream into a large mixing bowl. Whip the cream with the electric mixer on medium speed until the cream is fluffy and stiff.

3. Use the rubber spatula to gently fold the pudding into the whipped cream. Fold in a little bit at a time so the cream stays airy and light.

4. Pour the raspberries, blueberries, and dark chocolate chips into the bowl.

5. Gently fold the berries and chocolate into the vanilla cream. Scoop the salad into serving bowls. If you'd like, top with a drizzle of caramel topping!

Strawberry Hazelnut Crepes

A crepe is a very thin pancake that originated in France. What other crepe fillings would you like to try?

Ingredients

1 tablespoon butter
⅓ cup flour
½ cup milk
1 egg
salt
hazelnut spread
sliced strawberries

Supplies

microwave-safe dish
mixing bowl
whisk
measuring cups
nonstick skillet
spatula
plate
spoon
knife and cutting board

1. Place the butter in the microwave-safe dish. Microwave the butter 10 seconds at a time until it is melted. Let the butter cool.

2. In the mixing bowl, whisk together the flour, milk, egg, melted butter, and a pinch of salt until the mixture is smooth.

3. Heat the nonstick skillet on the stove over medium heat.

4. Pour ¼ cup of batter into the skillet. Then tilt the skillet so the batter spreads into a thin circle.

5. After about 30 seconds, flip the crepe with the spatula. Cook for 30 more seconds. Then transfer the crepe to the plate.

6. Gently spread a spoonful of hazelnut spread over the crepe. Fold the crepe in half.

7. Repeat steps 4 through 6 until the batter is gone. Top your finished crepes with a drizzle of hazelnut spread and strawberry slices!

Peach Grahams

These sweet dessert squares are like cheesecakes in simple snack form. No forks needed!

Ingredients

1 peach
1 teaspoon sugar
¼ teaspoon cinnamon
¼ cup soft cream cheese
1 teaspoon powdered sugar
2 tablespoons vanilla yogurt
graham crackers

Supplies

peeler or paring knife
knife and cutting board
microwave-safe bowl
mixing bowls
measuring cups and spoons
spoon
whisk
spreading knife

1. Peel and slice the peach. Place the slices into the microwave-safe bowl. In a small mixing bowl, combine the sugar and cinnamon.

2. Sprinkle the cinnamon sugar over the peaches and stir. Microwave the peaches for 30 seconds. Stir the peaches and set them aside.

3. In a medium mixing bowl, combine the cream cheese and powdered sugar until the mixture is smooth and creamy. Then whisk in the vanilla yogurt until smooth.

4. Spread 1 tablespoon of the cream cheese filling onto a graham cracker square. Then top the square with peach slices.

5. Repeat step 4 until the filling and peaches are gone. If you only want to make one or two grahams, store the rest of the filling and peaches separately in the refrigerator.

Banana Sushi

This dessert sushi mimics the real thing with crispy rice cereal and fun fruit toppings!

Food Fact!

Most real sushi is made with rice and fish. In this recipe, the sliced mango represents raw fish. The raspberry represents fish eggs!

Ingredients

½ cup crispy rice cereal
1 banana
nut butter
mango, peach, or apricot
raspberries

Supplies

measuring cup
plate
spreading knife
knife and cutting board
serving plate

1. Pour the crispy rice cereal onto the plate and spread it out.

2. Peel the banana. Use the spreading knife to cover the banana with nut butter.

3. Roll the banana over the crispy rice cereal until the banana is covered.

4. Slice the banana into pieces about ¾ inch (2 cm) thick.

5. Top each banana piece with a thin slice of mango, peach, or apricot and one quarter of a raspberry. Present your banana sushi slices in a row on the serving plate!

Cookies 'n' Cream Fluff

Calling all chocolate lovers! This rich pudding fluff is bursting with creamy, crunchy cocoa.

Ingredients

10 to 12 chocolate
    sandwich cookies
1½ cups milk
3.4-ounce package
    instant chocolate
    pudding mix
1¼ cups heavy cream

Supplies

sealable plastic bag
rolling pin or soup can
mixing bowls
measuring cups
whisk
electric mixer
rubber spatula
serving bowl

1. Place the chocolate sandwich cookies in the plastic bag. Seal the bag. Use the rolling pin or soup can to roll over the cookies and crush them into crumbs. Set the bag aside.

2. In a mixing bowl, combine the milk with the pudding mix. Whisk until the mixture gets thick. Put the bowl in the refrigerator while you whip the cream.

3. Pour the heavy cream into a large mixing bowl. Whip the cream with the electric mixer on medium speed until the cream is fluffy and stiff.

4. Use the rubber spatula to gently fold the cream into the chocolate pudding.

5. Pour the crushed chocolate cookies into the bowl. Use the spatula to gently fold the crumbs into the chocolate cream.

6. Scoop the fluff into the serving bowl. If you'd like, top with a chocolate sandwich cookie or cookie crumbs!

Jammy Wafers

A dusting of powdered sugar makes these sweet sandwiches extra dainty.

Ingredients

¼ cup cream cheese
1½ tablespoons powdered
  sugar
1 teaspoon milk
vanilla wafer cookies
¼ cup jam

Supplies

small bowl
measuring cups and
  spoons
spoon
spreading knife
plate or tray
mesh sifter

1. In the small bowl, mix the cream cheese, 1 tablespoon powdered sugar, and milk until smooth and creamy.

2. Spread 1 heaping teaspoon of the sweetened cream cheese over the bottom of a vanilla wafer cookie.

3. Spread 1 teaspoon jam over the bottom of another cookie.

4. Sandwich the cookies together. Place the sandwich on the plate or tray.

5. Repeat steps 2 through 4 to make more wafer sandwiches.

6. Scoop ½ tablespoon powdered sugar into the mesh sifter. Hold the sifter over the wafer sandwiches and gently tap it to cover the wafers with a light dusting of sugar. Then dig into your sweet and fruity treats!

Caramel Pretzel Milkshake

This frosty ice cream treat is
sweet, creamy, salty, and crunchy.

Ingredients

5 or 6 scoops vanilla ice cream

1 tablespoon caramel topping, plus extra for serving

½ cup pretzels, plus a few for serving

½ cup milk

whipped cream

Supplies

serving glass

ice cream scoop or large spoon

blender

measuring cups and spoons

1. Place the serving glass in the freezer while you prepare the milkshake.

2. Put the vanilla ice cream, caramel topping, pretzels, and milk in the blender.

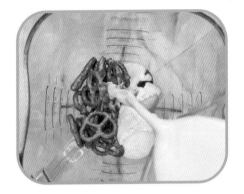

3. Blend everything together until the milkshake is smooth and creamy.

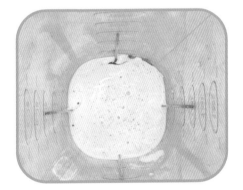

4. Take the serving glass out of the freezer and pour the milkshake into it. Top your milkshake with whipped cream, caramel topping, and pretzels!

More QUICK
Creative Fun!

10-MINUTE
PROJECTS

65 Projects You Can Make in a Flash

BY SARAH L. SCHUETTE

10-MINUTE
FUN and EASY
PROJECTS

65 Craft Activities
You Can Make
in a Flash

by Christopher Harbo, Sarah L. Schuette,
and Tammy Enz
illustrated by Lucy Makuc

Dabble Lab is published by Capstone Press, an imprint of Capstone.
1710 Roe Crest Drive, North Mankato, Minnesota 56003
capstonepub.com

Library of Congress Cataloging-in-Publication Data is available on the Library of Congress website.
ISBN 9781669078463 (paperback)
ISBN 9781669078470 (ebook PDF)

Summary: You're feeling hungry, but you're in a hurry. What do you do? Become a 15-minute foodie and whip up an easy, tasty dish. This collection of recipes for parties, snacks, meals, and desserts is perfect for kid cooks, and they'll be ready to serve in 15 minutes or less. Using basic kitchen supplies and techniques and step-by-step instructions, young chefs will be serving up something delicious in no time at all!

Image Credits
Capstone: Mighty Media, Inc.: project photos, supplies; Getty Images: andresr, 4, baibaz, cover, 7, 54, 55, 83 (fruit), Bozena_Fulawka, 53 (peppers), Dmytro, 45 (chickpeas), elena_hramowa, 93 (cookies), Floortje, 43 (grater and cheese), Inna Tarasenko, 63 (tomatoes), kolesnikovserg, 87 (apple slices), Natalia Samorodskaia, 57 (banana slices), RomarioIen, 51 (oat flakes), threeart, 61, 93, 109 (pretzels), unalozmen, 36, 37 (chocolate chips), VioletaStoimenova, 5

Design Elements
Getty Images: Sirintra_Pumsopa, yugoro

Editorial Credits
Editor: Jessica Rusick
Designer: Sarah DeYoung

About the Author

Megan Borgert-Spaniol is an author and editor of children's media. When she isn't writing or reading, she enjoys doing yoga, baking cookies, and crafting homemade pizzas. Megan lives in Minneapolis with a tall, goofy man and small, chatty cat.

Printed and bound in China. 5834